THE HARPERCOLLINS

POLITICAL
PAMPHLETEER

WOMEN AND POLITICS

PIPPA NORRIS
Harvard University

THE HARPERCOLLINS POLITICAL PAMPHLETEER, *WOMEN AND POLITICS,* Pippa Norris

Copyright © 1995 HarperCollins College Publishers

ISBN: 0-673-99779-0

98 9 8 7 6 5 4 3 2

INTRODUCTION

The fight for women's equal participation in politics has been an integral part of the struggle for democracy in America. The first battle, for women to gain equal citizenship rights, was won with passage of the Nineteenth Amendment in 1919. During the 1960s the revival of the women's movement centered around different issues on the political agenda: equal pay, sex discrimination, affirmative action, family policy, reproductive rights, sexual choice.

Under the Clinton administration, the emphasis shifted towards increasing the representation of women in the corridors of power, from the State House to the White House. There has been some success in developing an administration which 'looks more like America', and electing more women to office, nevertheless at the same time opponents of the women's movement became more assertive in the backlash against feminism.

The aim of this pamphlet is to outline the development of the women's movement in the United States and to assess in the 1990s how far women have achieved their goals.

This pamphlet will consider four main issues:

I. What is 'the women's movement'?

II. How do we explain developments in the first wave women's movement in America from 1840 to 1920.

III. How do we explain developments in the second wave women's movement since the 1960s?

IV. What have been the principle issues for women's representation during the 1990s?

I. What is 'the women's movement'?

The term 'women's movement' will be understood to mean the collective activities of those working for 'feminist' goals. As such it will be understood as a broad and eclectic movement including large well-organized campaigning groups, such as the National Abortion Rights League (NARAL), the National Organization of Women (NOW), and the National Women's Political Caucus (NWPC), but also more smaller more ad-hoc community groups such as local Women's Arts Collectives, and also traditional women's groups which are primarily social, although they may occasionally have a campaigning role, and may provide an avenue for women's participation in public life.

Although we often talk about the women's movement there are many groups, which come together in a loose alliance or coalition, with diverse concerns. In this sense it is unlike the trade union movement, with formal conditions of membership and a hierarchical and bureaucratic organization. Groups within the women's movement are divided by many factors: strategy and tactics, ideology and policy concerns, as well as race, region, class and sexual choice.

Like other social movements, the development of feminism can be seen as broadly cyclical, with periodic changes in the level of grassroots support and activism depending on the development of new issues, leadership, organizational divisions and political circumstances. In other words, even during periods of quiescence, such as the 1930s and early 1940s, the women's movement has never been wiped off the historical map. Indeed the women's movement may be more effective during quieter periods, when activity focuses on discrete lobbying, insider negotiations, and implementing legislation, rather than during periods of large-scale street demonstrations well-publicized in the media.

Moreover, the women's movement takes many different forms, with alternative concerns, in different countries. For example abortion laws were passed in the 1930's in many Scandinavian countries, in the 1960's in Britain, in the late 1970's in Italy, while in 1992 abortion remains illegal in Ireland. The political culture, party system, electoral system and policy agenda explain much of the crossnational variation.

In the development of any social movement we need to distinguish between two types of factors.

Background factors are enabling conditions such as social, ideological or economic change, which are necessary but not sufficient causes for the development of the women's movement. For example, the growth of the 'New Left' in the early 60s produced a radical challenge to many established ideas on issues like civil rights, the war in Vietnam and the 'War on Poverty'. Nevertheless these radical ideas did not influence the growth of the women's movement until these issues connected directly to concerns about women's equality. To take another instance, the number of women at work grew rapidly during the 1950s, but this was not linked to an active campaign for equal pay until women became organized on this issue, legislation was passed in 1963, and test cases were taken to court.

In contrast **proximate events** are specific precipitating or catalytic events, leaders or organizations, which build on the background conditions. For example, the publication of Betty Friedan's <u>The Second Sex</u> in 1963 was influential because it spoke to well-educated women who experienced the frustrations of middle class affluent lifestyles in their own lives.

II. In this light, how do we explain the rise and decline of the first wave women's movement from 1840 to 1920? What was its impact?

The American women's movement started in the 1840s with a broad range of concerns, before focusing almost exclusively towards the end of the century on the issue of female suffrage[1]. At least five background factors facilitated the growth of the first wave movement in the United States:

Background Factors:

The structural roots of women's mobilization can be traced to the process of industrialization and urbanization in the 19th century. The move from agrarian to industrial production had different consequences for middle and working class women. The main change was to reinforce the division between paid employment and work within the domestic sphere. Many middleclass women, who had previously worked on the family farm, lost their directly productive role. Instead their activity came to focus exclusively within the household. The reproductive role was also undermined, as large families were no longer economically valuable. Women gained leisure for voluntary activity. In addition the 'cult of true womanhood' reinforced and glorified the new role of domesticity. For working class women, in urban sweatshops, factories or domestic labor, industrialization reinforced the division between their home life and economic work.

At a time when many middle-class women lost their economic role, they gained new work through organizing a variety of voluntary groups, notably charity associations, religious revivals, benevolent associations, the temperance movement and Protestant non-conformist quakers. The bonds of organized religion allowed women to participate in the public sphere. Charitable work was seen as socially acceptable, since it provided a logical extension of women's domestic role, for example the temperance movement aimed to defend the home, protect the family, and strengthen moral virtues.

Of all the proximate causes identified in the origins of the women's rights movement, the most common is the abolitionist movement. From the beginning, many non-confederate women wanted to participate in the anti-slavery movement but were marginalised. At the World Anti-Slavery Convention in London in 1840, women delegates of the American Society found themselves excluded from an active role, they were not recognized or seated. This highlighted the contradictions in their position. Through the movement women gained experience of organization, oratorical skills, leadership and social consciousness. It provided resources for the mobilization of women's rights, and, to a lesser extent, consciousness of their own oppression.

Moreover, in the United States traditionally there has been a strong emphasis on Lockian liberalism and the belief in formal Constitutional Rights, including the right to life, liberty and the pursuit of happiness. In contrast with most European countries, America experienced a long tradition of democracy and the universal male franchise for the non-slave population. This seemed to highlight obvious contradictions for the position of women as citizens in America.

In addition, in the United States there was also a strong tradition of independent women owning property and farms , especially in the pioneering states such as Wyoming and Utah, which gave women the vote in the 1890s. Again this seemed to pose contradictions for many women who could own property, pay taxes, and yet be excluded from the franchise. Accordingly as a result of these factors the first wave women's movement developed, in different stages.

Precipitating Events:

The earliest history of the American women's movement can be traced to the famous conference at Seneca Falls in 1848, led by Elizabeth Cady Stanton and Lucretia Mott. Before the Civil War there were a series of conventions and informal networks, but no formal organization devoted exclusively to women's rights. The main focus of women's activity lay within the abolitionist movement. The first generation of feminists defined the problem of women in the widest sense - in social relationships, economic institutions, marriage and domesticity[2]. Hence the Seneca Falls Convention agreed to a series of demands including:

- property rights in all states for married women
- access to education and professional training
- the right to vote

Following the American Civil War the movement came to focus increasingly on the vote. If movements are defined on the basis of independent organizations, the women's movement came together under two banners in 1969.

- The National American Women's Suffrage Association (NASA) was formed under the leadership of Elizabeth Cady Stanton and Susan B. Anthony, with aims which were seen as fairly radical for the time, traced woman's oppression to marriage and the sexual division of labor.

- The American Women's Suffrage Association was also formed in 1869, under the leadership of Lucy Stone. This was more conservative with the main aim restricted to the right to vote.

Yet at the time these organizations were formed, the opportunity for change were receding. The demand for women's suffrage came to be independent of the abolitionist movement. In 1869 they proposed the 16th Amendment, extending the vote to women, modelled on the 15th amendment which extended the vote to black males. The period 1870-1890 saw the emergence of a diverse array of women's organizations, often based on social feminism. This refers to a range of causes often indifferent to the suffrage, such as the temperance movement. The women's rights movement declined somewhat in the late 1870's and 80's, except for some national conventions and lobbying.

After the resounding defeat of the suffrage amendment on the Senate floor in 1887, the two separate suffrage organizations decided to merge, with the formation of the National American Women Suffrage Association (NASA) in 1890. The new movement worked on state legislatures, gaining the vote in four western states between 1890-1896 (Wyoming, Colorado, Utah and Idaho). The main development affecting the movement were the widening of its social base, from the narrowly middle class organization towards more working class women, including stronger links with the Women's Trade Union League. Gradually the franchise was extended in other states: Washington in 1910, California in 1911, Arizona, Kansas and Oregon in 1912, and Illinois in 1913. Yet the eastern and Midwestern states mostly proved intractable, and considerable opposition came from liquor interests.

In 1913 the women's movement refocussed again at the federal level, with a massive parade overshadowing President Wilson's inaugural. In 1914 the movement experienced a split, between the heterogeneous broad NAWSA and the small but well defined, effective and more militant Congressional Union, which eventually became the National Women's Party. By 1915 the women's movement was large and diverse - with a middle class leadership but members drawn from the upper class, working class, professional women, club women, immigrant women, and some black women (although some blatant discrimination within the organization persisted too). There was a broad coalition involving the progressive movement, the labor movement, and settlement work. Congressmen who did not support the suffrage were targeted in elections, not always successfully. The next tactical move by the NWP was to picket the White House in Jan 1917 demanding the right to vote, and criticizing Woodrow Wilson. The government's response to civil unrest during wartime was arrests, prison sentences and hunger strikes. The effect was to move suffrage onto the central agenda, and to highlight differences between the radical NWP and the moderate NAWSA.

As a combined result of these developments - NWP militancy, NAWSA moderation, success at state level, women's involvement in wartime work, and the shifting political opportunity structures, - the House eventually passed the women's suffrage (Nineteenth) amendment by a two-thirds majority on 10 Jan 1918, with ratification finalized on 26 August 1919. This was followed by a sweeping series of reforms in the 1920's, women were given jury rights, they were allowed to enter the civil service, states passed minimum wage laws and laws restricting child labor.

But during the 20's, shortly after they had achieved their main objective with the vote, the movement became divided about the direction of future goals. On the one side the League of Women Voters favored further constitutional reform, notably passage of the Equal Rights Amendment (ERA) - to guarantee that "equal rights under the law shall not be denied or abridged by the United States or by any state on account of sex." Others, notably the militant National Women's Party, wanted to focus on social concerns such as child labor laws and issues of pacifism. Politicians initially feared they would have to make concessions to win the 'women's vote' but in the first election in which women could participate, in 1923, it was found that only 35% of women turned out to vote, and women's votes were similar to men's, there was no distinct 'women's bloc'. Accordingly as a result of these developments, and internal divisions, the power of the movement declined until by the mid-20's it had almost disappeared as a national organized group.

III. How do we explain developments in the second wave women's movement since the 1960s?

It is hard to present an accurate picture of the second-wave women's movement which developed from the early 1960's onwards. Despite the central role of the National Organization of Women (NOW), the movement as a whole has always been a fairly diverse and incoherent development, with many different groups, branches, and factions loosely structured, highly decentralized, with different concerns and interests[3]. Nevertheless we can chronicle the main features of 'second wave' feminism, highlighting four major background factors in the United States from the mid fifties to the early sixties.

First there was the development of the civil rights movement in the mid-fifties, challenging established assumptions about racial politics, aiming for desegregation in schools and equal voting rights. Groups such as the NAACP used a variety of techniques of passive resistance under the leadership of Martin Luther King, although Black Power groups under Stokely Carmichael advocated more radical steps. This brought the issue of equal rights back onto the political agenda, provided experience for many white liberals who took part in the bussing protests, and provided parallels for the women's movement.

The early 60's also saw the development of the radical new left movement, a range of groups concerned with challenging the established status quo and the quiescent politics of the 1950's Eisenhower years. The new left was linked with civil rights and also concerned with issues of political participation, the rediscovery of poverty in the United States, the anti-Vietnam movement and the communitarian/hippie movement. By 1968 the women's movement was part of the expansion of direct action by students, blacks, and Democratic activists.

Thirdly there was a significant expansion of feminist literature. This includes the publication of Betty Friedan's seminal book *The Feminine Mystique* in 1963. The success of the book took the author and publisher by surprise - it seemed to touch a chord among a generation of suburban housewives. Friedan develops a critique of the predominant images of women as the 'happy housewife' generated by the media and advertising, reinforced by theories of Freudian psychology and functional analysis. For many women reading the book changed their lives, it seemed to set off a 'click' of consciousness, as they were able to make the connection between what they had seen as personal problems and issues common to all women. Questions which might have appeared trivial, - of how to cope with the isolation of suburban life, the boredom of domesticity and the problems of housework when they were told in the media and advertising that they should be able to achieve domestic happiness, - came to be seen as significant problems common to women as a group. Women need to talk, and to listen, to each other. Small groups and networks developed across the states concerned with consciousness raising, developing the idea that the 'personal is the political' and 'sisterhood is powerful'. As a result there were many other classic publications, such as Kate Millet's Sexual Politics in 1970, and the explosion of courses in women's studies in universities.

In addition, there were legislative moves. President Kennedy initiated the Presidential Commission on the Status of Women in 1963, which raised issues of civil and political rights, childcare, education and taxes.

In 1963 Congress passed the Equal Pay Act which was designed to achieve equal pay for men and women doing the same work in the same establishment.

At the same time 1964 Title VII of the Civil Rights Act, was designed to prevent discrimination on the basis of sex, as well as race, color or national origin. The Act prohibited discrimination in many aspects of work - hiring, firing, promotion and benefits by employers, unions and employment agencies. It is worth noting that sex was only included because a Southern Congressman, Howard Smith, in an attempt to wreck the bill and increase opposition. The Equal Employment Opportunity Commission gave little attention to enforcing and implementing the act for women in the early years. It was a long a difficult legal struggle to prove rights had been denied.

In 1967 there was also the Executive Order on Affirmative Action: major government contractors had to develop affirmative action programs and set goals for overcoming discrimination where women and ethnic minorities were underrepresented. Employers had to produce a timetable of progress for change in recruitment, hiring and training, although there were problem about enforcement and compliance.

Precipitating Events:

These background factors interrelated with certain precipitating events.

Following the grassroots success of the consciousness raising groups, and regional meetings, in 1966 Betty Friedan founded NOW, the National Organization of Women, which remains the main organization of the American movement. The movement expanded rapidly in grassroots support, local chapters and public meetings in the next few years. To summarize its goals in 1967 NOW demanded an eight point plan:

1. An equal rights constitutional amendment (ERA)
2. Enforcement of the law banning sex discrimination.
3. Maternity employment rights
4. Tax deduction for home and childcare expenses
   for working parents.
5. Child day care centers.
6. Equal and non-segregated education
7. Equal Job Training opportunities
8. The right of women to control their reproductive lives.

The demand for the legalization of abortion proved controversial and divisive, as did the issue of lesbianism and sexual choice in later meetings. Membership of NOW increased from 1122 and 14 chapters in 1967 to its peak of 220,000 members, with an annual budget of $14 million, in 1982. To publicize their case NOW organized direct action demonstration, notably in 1968 at the Miss America Pageant in Atlantic City where women dumped bras and girdles into a 'freedom trash bucket'. The late sixties saw the development of more radical feminist groups, notably the Redstockings of New York, who favored small-group consciousness raising, women's collectives, grassroots agitation and direct action at the community level.

In 1973 abortion was legalized in the landmark case in the Supreme Court, Roe v.Wade, by the Supreme Court. In part in reaction to this decision, the pro-life forces increased in strength, such as the Hyde Amendment in 1975 which restricted the use of federal funds for abortion services. From the mid-seventies onwards the conservative backlash gained momentum, notably the campaign of the Moral Majority led by Jerry Falwell and Phyllis Schlafly, so that women became more concerned about defending the rights they had achieved through lobbying and legal action that with making further dramatic gains.

In the mid and late seventies NOW focussed considerable energies on the attempted passage of ERA, the Equal Rights Amendment to the constitution first submitted to Congress in 1923. After an immense lobbying effort the amendment was passed by the House in October 1971, followed by the Senate a year later. Unfortunately, despite an extensive nation-wide campaign, the pro-ERA lobby failed to secure ratification in two-thirds of all states by the required deadline of June 1982.

During the mid to late eighties attention focussed on a range of campaigns: further legislation to secure 'equal pay for equal worth'; test cases in affirmative action at work; moves to increase the number of women in state-wide and national elective office, following the emergence of the 'gender gap'; concern about social policies to reverse trends towards the 'feminization of poverty'; demands for increased protection against domestic violence at home and sexual harassment at work; and campaigns to secure maternity leave and childcare facilities.

Accordingly the women's movement demonstrated it had evolved over the years, experiencing periods of success and failure on different campaigns, but the issues raised by the movement remain as vital today to the debate in American democracy as during its peak in the sixties.

IV. What have been the principle issues for women's representation during the 1990s?

In the early nineties concern about reproductive rights and sexual harassment stimulated a resurgence of public support for the women's movement. The Supreme Court appointments of President Reagan and President Bush shifted the judicial tide in a more conservative direction. The women's movement became concerned with protecting the reproductive rights it had achieved, threatened by the 1989 Supreme Court decision to allow states to regulate abortion in Webster v. Missouri. Some blocking demonstrations by the Christian Right, as well as well-publicized cases of violence against providers of abortion services, fuelled further fears about access to reproductive rights. Moreover in Senate hearings charges by Anita Hill against the nomination to the Supreme Court of Justice Thomas Clarence, in October 1991, dramatically raised the issue of sexual harassment. The

'Tail-hook' scandal in the navy further publicized this problem.

The Senate hearings, combined with the Webster case, re-energized the movement, bringing together a diverse coalition of older feminists and younger activists to support record numbers of women candidates for the House and Senate in the 1992 election. The focus for much activity in the early 1990s has been mobilizing the increased power of women, whether expressed through the ballot box or through election to office.

The 'gender gap' in voting first became widely noted in the 1980 Presidential election. This election signified a critical realignment in American gender politics, that is, a significant shift in voting choice and party identification which has subsequently been consolidated over successive elections. The development of the 'gender gap' represents a long-term, decisive change in the party loyalties of women and men, with significant consequences for electoral competition, for the political mobilization of women, and for the salience of gender issues on the public policy agenda.

In the early eighties three developments generated concern about the gender gap in American elections: for the first time, more women than men voted, they voted in a distinctive way, and the women's movement seized on these trends to advance their agenda. In the 1980 and 1984 elections the gender gap could be dismissed as a short-term reaction to President Reagan's leadership and the mobilization of the new right. But trends since then, with American women consistently leaning more heavily towards the Democrats while men favored the Republicans, convinced even the most skeptical observer that this was not merely a temporary blip.

The first significant trend was the greater mobilization of women voters. For successive decades since 1920, when the franchise was first granted, women had slightly lower levels of turnout. According to data from the US Bureau of the Census, differences in participation gradually diminished over time in America, as in many other countries. The 1980 election saw parity in turnout. In successive elections since then women have participated at slightly higher rates than men (see Figure 1). The percentage difference is not great but it is politically significant. Combined with patterns of longevity, and age-related turnout, women heavily out-number men voters. In the 1992

12

presidential election, about 45.3m women cast their ballots compared with 38.6m men.

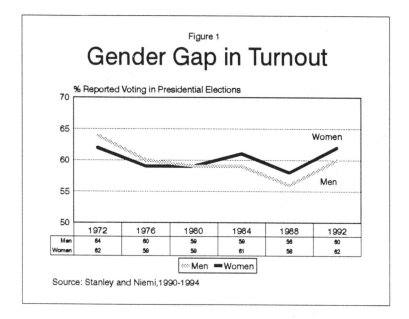

Figure 1

Gender Gap in Turnout

% Reported Voting in Presidential Elections

	1972	1976	1980	1984	1988	1992
Men	64	60	59	59	56	60
Women	62	59	59	61	58	62

�·�·�·Men ▬Women

Source: Stanley and Niemi,1990-1994

The second major trend in the 1980s was the shift in voting choice and party identification among the American electorate. There had long been gender differences in party support. In the classic work *The Political Role of Women* published in 1955, Maurice Duverger found women voters slightly more right-wing than men in Norway, France, and Germany[4].

During the 1960s Randall suggests in most countries women voters were consistently more conservative than men by a small margin, according to the available evidence [5]. Women's conservatism was commonly explained by their greater longevity and religiosity, and their lower trade union membership, rather than by gender per se [6]. Similar trends were evident in the United States. As Campbell et al noted, in the 1952-1960 presidential elections women were slightly more Republican than men, in the region of 3-5 percent, although this could be attributed to differences in age, regional turnout, and education [7]. The NES data was confirmed by Gallup polls which

13

registered stronger female support for the Republican Presidential candidate in every election during the 1950s [8].

During the 1960s and 1970s the voting difference between women and men, reported in surveys, were usually statistically insignificant (see Figure 2). The gender gap in voting became evident in 1980; since then American women have consistently given stronger support to Democratic candidates. As a result in the 1992 contest, according to the exit poll, women plumped 46:37 per cent in favor of Clinton over Bush, while men split by a far narrower margin of 41:38 per cent. Similar trends are evident at all other levels of elected office[9].

Evidence for gender realignment is confirmed by trends in partisanship. From 1952-1970 there were women and men has largely similar party loyalties. In contrast, from 1972 male support for the Democrats started to decline, producing a gender difference which expanded in the 1980s. In the 1992 election, 33 per cent of men were self-identified Democrats, compared with 39 per cent of women [10].

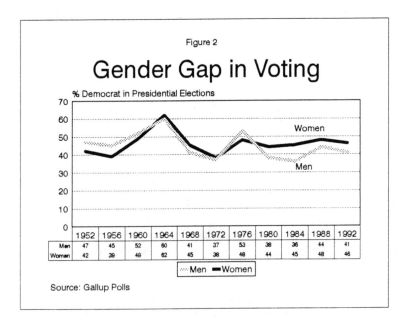

Figure 2

Gender Gap in Voting

% Democrat in Presidential Elections

	1952	1956	1960	1964	1968	1972	1976	1980	1984	1988	1992
Men	47	45	52	60	41	37	53	38	36	44	41
Women	42	39	49	62	45	38	48	44	45	48	46

···· Men ■ Women

Source: Gallup Polls

The third important development was the way the organized feminist movement, women party activists, and women politicians, seized on this trend to advance their agenda, and how this influenced patterns of party competition [11]. As a result of publicizing this issue, press coverage of the gender gap expanded dramatically in the early 1980s, reaching its peak in 1994, before subsiding. The gender gap in most presidential and congressional elections has not been great, - in the region of 4 to 10 percentage points, - but it has been politically significant. Why? The women's movement mobilized around this development, it affects millions of votes, these votes are dispersed across every electoral district, the gender gap cannot be explained (and therefore modified) by a single issue, and it is a relatively recent phenomenon. As a result parties have sought to compete for women's ballot box power, with only a hazy understanding of what steps are necessary to retain or regain women's votes.

1992: The Year of the Woman Politician?

The realignment of electoral politics led by fits and starts towards the 1992 election, dubbed the 'Year of the Woman' by popular commentator, once politicians awoke to the political salience of gender at the ballot box[12]. In 1992 the success of Democratic women in Senate and House races was combined with the election of Bill Clinton, a President committed to a more diverse administration. More women than ever before were appointed to high cabinet and executive office, including the heads of the Departments of Energy, Health and Human Services, and Justice. Women held posts as U.N. Ambassador, head of the Environmental Protection Agency and chair of the Council of Economic Advisors. Nevertheless there were indications that 1992 represented a temporary peak, which would not always be replicated in subsequent elections. Moreover, the representation of women in American politics continued to lag far behind the position in many other democracies.

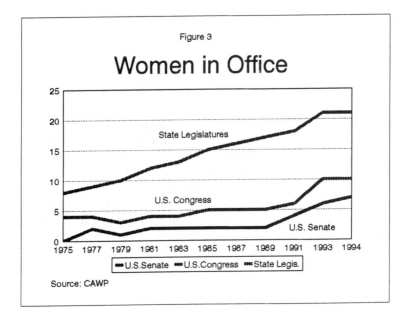

Figure 3

Women in Office

Source: CAWP

The 'year of the woman' referred mainly to dramatic gains on Capital Hill. From 1990-1992 the number of women who won major party nominations in House primaries jumped from 69 to 106. Even more importantly, in 1992 the number of women representatives in the House rose dramatically to 48 out of 435 members (including one delegate for Washington D.C.). Women represent 10.8 percent of House members in 1992, up from 6.4 per cent in 1990. Female members are a diverse group ethnically and regionally, from twenty-seven states, although there is less balance in party terms, since thirty-five are Democrats.

In 1992 records were also broken in the Senate, where eleven women ran, and six won. The four new Senators included Barbara Boxer and Dianne Feinstein for California, the first state to return two women, the first black woman Senator, Carol Moseley-Braun (D-Ill), and Patty Murray (D-Wash) who ran as a 'mom in tennis shoes'. In June 1993 they were joined by another woman who won a special election, Kay Bailey Hutchinson (R-Tx). In 1994 Dianne Feinstein had to defend her seat against tough competition from Michael Huffington, while three Republican women contested Senate seats: Kay Bailey Hutchinson in

16

Texas, Olympia Snowe in Maine and Jan Stoney in Nebraska.

Part of the reason for progress on Capital Hill is the gradual and steady expansion of the pool of eligible women politician with experience of state and local office. From 1975-94, the number of women in county governing office quadrupled, from 450 to 1653, or 9 per cent[13]. Female city mayors increased; in January 1994, among the 100 largest cities in the U.S, 18 have women mayors including San Diego CA, San Jose CA, Washington D.C., Fort Worth TX, Portland OR, Pittsburgh PA, Las Vegas NV and Tampa FL. If we compare all cities with populations over 30,000, 18 per cent have women mayors.

At state level there has also been steady and continuous progress (see Diagram 4). In 1994 there were women governors in Kansas (Joan Finney), Texas (Ann Richards), New Jersey (Christine Todd Whitman) and Oregon (Barbara Roberts), while eleven women were lieutenant governors, and eight were attorney generals. Between 1975 and 1994 the number of women in state legislatures more than doubled, from 604 to 1,516 (from 8 to 21 percent). Female representation varies significantly from state to state; it is strongest (about one third) in Arizona, Maine, Colorado, New Hampshire, Vermont, and Washington while it is weakest in Louisiana (2%), Kentucky (5%) and Alabama (6%), Arkansas (7%) and Mississippi (7%).
The gradual expansion of the pool of eligible women meant that if good opportunities arose then more were in positions to run for office. Nevertheless change in Congress remains slow because of the structure of opportunities for politicians within the American political system. Institutional factors which determine these opportunities include the role of parties, PACs, the media, rates of incumbency turnover and the electoral system.

Parties

In the past many believe that the traditional attitudes of party leaders were a barrier to women. But in more recent years studies suggest that parties have changed, and national party organizations have played more of an advocate role for women in office [14]. In the last decade parties have taken active steps to promote women's candidacies, including national conferences for female party activists to urge them to run for office, special funds targeted for women party candidates, training seminars, and positive statements in party platforms. Why? Women have gradually taken over many leadership positions within parties, which has changed the organization from within. Even more importantly, recruiting women candidates has been perceived as good electoral politics in recent years. The gender gap has highlighted the advantage of women candidates who can attract cross-over votes. Moreover, women challengers were seen as attractive to voters given the strong tide against incumbents, and the perception of women politician as 'outsiders'.

Nevertheless the positive role of American parties is limited, compared with other democracies. The Democrats and Republicans are weak organizations with little influence over the recruitment process, and therefore they cannot play a central role in determining the choice of party candidates. Parties are especially weak in the pre-primary stage, since they are reluctant to provide early funding.

PACS and Money

The decline of parties has seen the rise of Political Action Committees as key gatekeepers. In the past it was believed that money was an obstacle for women, who were thought to lack the business and social networks necessary for fundraising. Yet most recent studies have found that women have done as well as men in raising money, once we control for the type of candidacy: whether incumbent, open race, or challenger [15]. Indeed the success of PACs developed specifically to funnel more money into the early stages of women's races, such as Emily's List, gave women candidates a financial advantage in 1992. Emily's List was founded in 1982 to give women financial resources in the early stages of fundraising, which are critical for candidate credibility - EMILY stands for Early Money is Like Yeast. The group solicits and bundles the money, and it has become a powerful force. In 1990 it raised $1.5 million for 14 candidates - of whom nine won. More generally there were thirty-five PACs in 1992 which either gave money predominantly to women candidates, or had a mainly female donor base.

The Media

The media represent another key player, since candidates convey their message through paid advertising and news coverage of the campaign. Studies of media coverage of US Senate candidates have found that male and female politicians are treated differently by the press, but it is less clear what consequences this has on electoral behavior[16]. Generally it has been found that women candidates receive less coverage in the news - regardless of their status. This may hurt women's chances of election if this inhibits vote's name recognition. Reporters also give more attention to negative campaign resources for women - their lack of endorsements or funding - even when controlling for the type of race. In addition, studies have found there was an emphasis on different issues for male and female candidates: more coverage of women candidates was devoted to so called 'female issues' (such as childcare, the environment or social programs) . In contrast men were given greater coverage on the issues of foreign policy, defense, and economics. Therefore the media may be a barrier for women but it may also be a resource, depending partly on the strategy of women candidates. In election campaigns focussed on debates about health care, unemployment and family leave, the gender stereotypes in the media, which reflect those in society, may be an advantage for women. On the other hand if the critical issue agenda is dominated by concerns about American intervention in Haiti, the Gulf and Bosnia, or issues of crime and policing, then gender stereotypes may be positive for male candidates.

Conclusions: The Slow Pace of Change

We have seen that more women now form the pool of eligibles, with political experience which positions them to move up the political ladder. They do not appear to be at a disadvantage in fundraising, nor do parties provide a significant obstacle. Although the media treats women candidates through a gender frame, this does not necessarily prove negative. Particularly in contests focussing on such issues as welfare, education and family policy, the gender frame may serve to benefit women, who are perceived as more compassionate and caring. Yet as we have seen progress remains slow, particularly compared with countries like Finland, Sweden and the Netherlands, where women are now over one third of elected members in parliament.

The principle reasons why progress is not faster in the United States are the electoral system (plurality single member districts) combined with are the electoral system (plurality single member districts) combined with the rate of incumbency turnover. Comparative research has found that women tend to be underrepresented in Anglo–American democracies using first–past– the–post, where candidates run in single member districts, rather than party list systems of proportional representation. The main reasons appear to be the electoral incentives facing parties, who know that they may lose votes if they do not include a balanced slate in party lists. In contrast in single member districts where selection is decided at local level there is no obligation, and often no clear mechanism, for parties to include equal proportions of men and women candidates.

In addition, slow rates of incumbency turnover provide a barrier to rapid change for any 'out' group. New members can enter Congress via three routes: through winning open seats where the previous member retired, through defeating the incumbent in primary elections within their party, or through challenging the incumbent in the November general election. One of the main reasons for women's gains in Congress in 1992 was the record number of representatives who were voluntarily retiring, as well as higher than average defeats in primaries. Normally we can expect about nine out of ten House members seeking reelection to be returned. As a result in 1992 there were 110 new members of the House and 11 new members of the Senate. Even if women were half the new members, and none of the retiring representatives, it would still require many successive elections before the US Congress started to 'look like America'.

About the Author

Pippa Norris is Associate Director of the Joan Shorenstein Center on the Press, Politics and Public Policy, and lecturer at the Kennedy School of Government, Harvard University. Her books include *Political Recruitment: Gender, Race and Class in the British Parliament; Different Roles, Different Voices: Women and Politics in the United States and Europe; Politics and Sexual Equality; British By–elections: The Volatile Electorate; Gender and Party Politics;* and successive editions of the *British Elections and Parties Yearbook.* She is currently editing new books on *Comparing Democratic Elections* and *Comparative Recruitment.* She has taught at Harvard, Edinburgh and Northumberland universities.

Endnotes

[1] For a detailed historic account of developments see Eleanor Flexnor *Century of Struggle* (Atheneum, New York, 1974); or Christine Bolt *The Women's Movements* (Harvester Wheatsheaf, Herts, 1993).

[2] For some of the ideas of the early feminists see Olive Banks *Faces of Feminism* (Blackwell, Oxford, 1986).

[3] For a readable account of the movement see Marcia Cohen *The Sisterhood* (Simon and Schuster, New York, 1988).

[4] Maurice Duverger *The Political Role of Women* (Paris: UNESCO, 1955).

[5] For a review see Vicky Randall *Women and Politics* 2nd Edition (London: Macmillan, 1987) pp68-78.

[6] Seymour Lipset *Political Man* (Garden City, N.J.: Doubleday, 1960).

[7] Angus Campbell, Philip E.Converse, Warren E.Miller and Donald E.Stokes *The American Voter* (New York, John Wiley & Sons, 1960) p.493.

[8] See also Emily Stoper 'The gender gap concealed and revealed: 1936-1984' Journal of Political Science 17 (1,2) Spring 1989, 50-62.

[9] For an analysis of the gender gap in 1990-92 Senate races, especially those with women candidates, see Elizabeth Adell Cook 'Voter Responses to Women Senate Candidates' in Elizabeth Adell Cook, Sue Thomas and Clyde Wilcox *The Year of the Woman: Myths and Realities* (Boulder, Co, Westview Press, 1994). For trends in Congressional voting see Harold W.Stanley and Richard G.Niemi *Vital Statistics on American Politics* (Washington DC, CQ Press, 1994) Table3-12 p109.

[10] Harold W.Stanley and Richard G.Niemi *Vital Statistics on American Politics* (Washington DC, CQ Press,1994) Table 5-2 p.161.

[11] See, for example, Kathy Bonk 'The Selling of the 'gender gap': The Role of Organized Feminism' in Carol M.Mueller *The Politics of the Gender Gap* (Newbury Park, Sage, 1988); Eleanor Smeal *Why and How Women will Elect the Next President* (New York, Harper Row, 1984); Linda Witt, Karen M.Paget and Glenna Matthews *Running as a Woman: Gender and Power in American Politics* (New York, Free Press, 1994), pp7-180.

[12] For more details on the 1992 races see Elizabeth Adell Cook, Sue Thomas and Clyde Wilcox (eds) *The Year of the Woman* (Westview Press, Boulder, Co., 1994).

[13] Figures are supplied by the Center for the American Woman in Politics, Rutgers University.

[14]See Barbara Burrell *A Woman's Place is in the House* (University of Michigan Press, Ann Arbor, 1994).

[15] Robert Darcy, Susan Welch and Janet Clark *Women, Elections and Representation* (University of Nebraska Press, 2nd edition, 1994).

[16]Kim Kahn and Edie N.Goldenberg 'Evaluations of Male and Female U.S.Senate candidates: An investigation of Media Influences' *Journal of Politics* 1994.

Questions for Thought:

1. What are the most important priorities for the women's movement in the 1990s?

2. Is the women's movement in decline today, with the development of a 'post-feminist' generation?

3. Has the American women's movement focussed too much energy on securing constitutional rights for women, rather than adequate social programs for the family and childcare?

4. How does the women's movement in the United States compare with similar movements in other countries?

5. Women continue to earn about 65c for every dollar that a man earns, in weekly hourly earnings before tax and benefits. What are the most effective strategies to change this?

6. Why are there so few women in Congress? Does it matter?